THOUGHT CATALOG BOOKS

The Art of Nostalgia

The Art of Nostalgia

LAUREN SUVAL

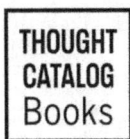

THOUGHT CATALOG Books

BROOKLYN, NY

THOUGHT CATALOG BOOKS

Copyright © 2016 by Lauren Suval

First edition, 2016

ISBN 978-1945796289

10 9 8 7 6 5 4 3 2 1

Cover photography and design by © KJ Parish

Contents

Nostalgic For My Old Summers

Growing up, summer meant that school was out, and all I really yearned to do was pretend that I was a version of Britney Spears, strolling along Rockaway Beach, singing the words to "Sometimes." I envisioned my life as a pop star. I'd make whimsical music videos on the beach and the waves would gently break at the shore. I'd sell out albums and concert tickets and date someone from a boy band. (Justin Timberlake—I was looking at you.) In this recurring fantasy of mine, I resided in a big house (painted in a sandy beige) that was situated on the dead-end of a winding road, sand dunes, and water right outside my door.

There were summer days and summer nights spent at an amusement park in Brooklyn. I used to be terrified of a statue of a large man with a black beard that stoically stood in the middle of the park. But then I'd ride an orange bus that lifted me up into the sky close to the clouds and then back down again, the speed increasing with each turn. It wasn't anything crazy, but for me, that was enough. After the ride was over, I'd devour a Firecracker popsicle, perfectly content to lick the red, white, and blue as the melted ice dripped down my neck and onto my bright green shorts.

———————

During the summers of my adolescence, my sixteen- and seventeen-year-old self clung to the notion of the waves. If you were to ask my boyfriend at the time, he would tell you that I was obsessed with the idea of floating like a mermaid. Why haven't I explored the water like that before? Was it a fear of drowning? Did I just assume pools were the only avenue for swimming? I recall the summer of 2006 when I was determined to be immersed in the ocean's lair. I wanted to move past the rocks and the awkward seaweed and float—I wanted to stand still for a goddamn minute. I closed my eyes and allowed the gentle rise and fall of the waves, along with the murmurs of its ebb and flow, swallow me whole. In that moment, I was abundantly and deliciously free.

My showers following my beach ventures were revitalizing in the best possible way. The scent of sunscreen and sea air still lingered on me, and I was happy when I noticed a burn on my body. My skin would darken, I thought. I'll look tan and experienced in summer's habitat.

———————

Old summers were filled with visits to my great-grandmother's at the Jersey Shore. They were comprised of teenage sound-tracks that featured Say Anything, Brand New, Gwen Stefani, The Black Eyed Peas, and (please don't hate me for saying this), Paris Hilton. (Remember "Stars are Blind?") Old summers tasted like cheap fried seafood and smelled like chlorine. Old summers looked like shimmering oceans at noon and cobalt blue skies at dusk. Old summers gave way to the freedom that comes with being a kid or a teenager.

———————

Summers now are saturated with skepticism; summers now embody a repulsion to the weather and incorporate a growing animosity towards the heat. When I was younger, I didn't give much thought to the hot temperatures—the intense humidity—but now they render headaches and nausea and lethargy. My mom says that people tend to care more when they get older.

———————

Summers now encompass that first jarringly hot day of the season. There was that time I was standing outside a cafe, stressed and run down with a cold and on the phone with my friend while slowly maneuvering my way to the parking lot. The sun beat down on me, but it was no friendly visitor. If the sun could talk, it would be most likely be taunting me like that popular girl who picked on me in middle school. It would most likely be making a mockery of my physical and emotional disposition, which was utterly exacerbated by the sun's snarky bite.

———————

Summers now feature less afternoons spent emulating a mermaid in the Atlantic and more days trying to sift my way through 'adulthood,' still encumbered in a transitional period filled with immediate unknowns.

———————

Old summers were coated in a particular brand of innocence, one that's been missing in my summers now.

And yet, even if summers now are no longer the same, when I stow away my bathing suits—my bathing suits with the smell of Banana Boat Lotion ingrained within the fabric—I'll savor its scent.

I know that in ten years, I'll think back to these summers, too.

Times At The Jersey Shore

I. My slippery fingers grab the edges of the in-ground pool as I dutifully tread water. The deep end tests my resiliency to stay afloat.

I stare at the male lifeguard, bronzed and mysterious under black shades. I can't decide whether he's legitimately apathetic or just bored. Probably the latter. I watch the interactions between him and the female lifeguards, formulating my own storylines for their lives, vicariously living through their flirtatious banter.

Not wanting to be too obvious, I return my attention to the blue water passing around and through me. I lie on my back, creating ripples with my hands, while I will any tension in my body to vanish.

When I step out of the pool, shivering until a towel eliminates the goosebumps on my skin, I peer out at the condominium where my great-grandmother stays for the summer. It's illuminated by the soft light of the sun. A slight breeze caresses my face, and I feel safe.

I've been coming here every summer. Every summer since I was a young girl.

———————

II. Tiny seashells are engrained within the scalding sand. The ground is rough on the feet, but it's worth it as I make my trek to the other side of the beach.

I think a lot on these walks. Reflective thoughts. Nice thoughts. The view, along with the sea air, helps heal wounds and encourages compassion. Compassion for myself—for heartache and stress and anxiety—for the human experience. Compassion for growth.

The wind howls through my hair that is frizzy and messy and wild.

———————

III. When the sun sets, I fidget with the squeaky sliding door to the porch and go outside, into the night. I like being on this small balcony alone; the balcony that overlooks the pitch-black ocean and all the twinkling lights that shine in the dark. I see the other condominium across the street. I see lights on in tiny windows, and I wonder what people are up to at this very moment. I inhale peace and exhale contentment.

IV. We drive through my great-grandmother's neighborhood, Deal. Deal is where Syrian Jews retreat for the summer. We drive through the tree-lined streets by the water. We pass the luxurious homes with stucco roofs, beautiful and expansive properties, and private pool clubs. We pass Sarah's Tent in town, the Syrian supermarket that sells the Bissli brand of onion rings I'm always eager to purchase.

I ask if we can drive through Asbury Park, a seaside community nearby and a staple to Jersey Shore history. Asbury Park is home to the Stone Pony, a historic music club, and a big boardwalk with rides and arcades.

Whenever I envision Asbury Park, I conjure up lyrics by Bruce Springsteen:

Down in town the circuit's full with switchblade lovers
so fast so shiny so sharp
As the wizards play down on Pinball Way on the boardwalk
way past dark
And the boys from the casino dance with their shirts open
like Latin lovers along the shore
Chasin' all them silly New York virgins by the score

Sandy, the aurora is risin' behind us
The pier lights our carnival life forever

Love me tonight for I may never see you again
Hey Sandy girl

My mother suggests that the 'boys from the casino' could be referencing the Syrian Jewish men in Deal. We aren't sure of course, but it's fun to speculate and to be in a place that upholds a certain kind of attachment. Even through song.

———————

As time passed, our own time at the Jersey Shore began to dwindle, little by little. Until nothing was left at all.

I still hold onto its fragments, though. I still hold onto its spirit, knowing that some things will not be forgotten.

3

We Didn't Have Time For Adulthood

It's so weird. I was little. And suddenly, I'm not little.
—Waiting For Forever

I. Teenage girls were scattered on the white rug in sleeping bags. Whispering. Story-telling when the lights went out. Breakfast in the morning featured gooey Cinnabons and sleepy eyes. Crust in the corners. Much-needed naps when we got home.

II. Drama club hosted tech nights on Fridays. Freshmen worked in the pit. I followed suit. With dread and curiosity. Move this piece of wood here, place these props for that show there. Idolizing the upperclassmen. Observing who is dating who. Which girls are role models. Which guys notice us.

III. Our feet dangled in the shallow end of the public pool, the public pool with the gated fence. Just another high school summer in suburbia. Belting out pop songs in the water while giggling. Taking photos for MySpace. Discussing upcoming classes. What this guy said in that online message. What was expressed in between the lines. Will he eventually try to hang out? For real?

IV. On the phone, we counted down the days until winter break. Vacation in the Catskill mountains. Anticipation for the resort, for every bite of food in the dining hall, for every snowy tube ride down the hill. Trying not to think about it being over before it began. Depressed when it was over.

V. Double dates were held at TGI Fridays. Too nervous to eat the chicken fingers in front of me. Butterflies swarmed my insides like an army ready to attack. Words etched the pages of my journal. Logging in details of my first everything. The kisses. The touches. The mundane. Today we had a blue Powerade in the park and held hands. Bubblegum poppy sap. Pre-broken heart. Pre 'pieces falling everywhere on the floor and it will take a very long time to pick up.'

VI. Chemistry homework after school was a drag. There were extensive research papers for English, citing sources and not forgetting to attach the bibliography at the end. Wore sweat pants on gym days to avoid the lockers. Avoided contact sports.

VII. Had journalism with a teacher who had a knack for dark humor. Reveled in his shenanigans. Had economics with a teacher who had a knack for corny humor. Reveled in his shenanigans while everyone else stared blankly.

VIII. Bells sounded in between periods. Lunch signaled a chance for the outside. Walk a few blocks from the school, feel the sunshine when you can. Cliques formulated. I was not in the popular one, but we had our own group, our own crew.

XI. Antsy for the weekends. For fried chicken salads with honey mustard at Applebees on Bedford Avenue. For lights of the movie theatre on a Friday night. For malls, not for shopping, but for roaming and browsing and chatting. High school kids were running around like mad, but we never strayed outside the lines.

X. We were shielded from what was ahead. Content in our blissful ignorance. We didn't have time for adulthood. We had quizzes in history class. We had July and August to be silly and carefree, and we knew where we'd be come fall—encumbered in a non-gray space. But maybe, just maybe, we knew that we could still retain some of our childish naiveté, even if there were scraps we can never get back.

4

Getaways At The Catskill Mountains

I complain about my frailty while trekking uphill, or I moan that my leg muscles ache. But it's a playful kind of whining—the kind where you don't take whatever it is too seriously. You're almost there, they say. I grip the snow tube's handles, mumbling that I better not tumble off the path. The ride down is fast and cold as the wind screams and the air hits my face. It's over before I know it, and I shriek with amusement while getting up to do it again.

———

My family, along with family friends, go to the Catskills every February. The latest resort on our radar is Kutshers in Monticello.

When we arrive, it feels like we never left. We see the spacious lobby with armchairs and comfy couches and warm colored tapestries near the fireplace. The lobby is the communal ground for vacationers yearning to escape reality—even for just a little bit.

Once we're settled into our rooms, we're given a schedule of the weekend's activities. The indoor pool is open late and mountains of snow are outside for tubing and skiing and snowmobiling. There's an older woman with dark lipstick and bold eye shadow in the lobby after breakfast offering makeovers. There's a game of Simon Says for the small children.

My favorite daytime activity, the daily bingo game, is conducted by a man with a bellowing voice. The kind you'd hear on television. Or maybe even in theatre. And even though I don't win the cash prize, I find the bingo games to be strangely calming. Maybe it's the comfort I find in tradition; when we go to Kutshers, we always play bingo.

And then there's the arcade, also open late. I gravitate towards the driving game. I drive all over the country, Hawaii and California and other locations that are foreign to me. People crowd around, relaying how they're frightened for my future license since I tend to knock things down. I try to reassure them, of course, but I continue to drive recklessly, determined to advance my placement. I'm on the parkway, navigating my way through various twists and turns. I suppose driving is sort of like life.

———

We dress up Saturday night for dinner. Saturday night is why my mother reminds me to pack something black, something uppity and fitting. I fuss over my thick curls and carefully apply a coat of pale pink gloss on my lips in the fluorescently-lit bathroom.

Cocktail hour features hors d'oeuvres in the night club before we join everyone in the dining room. There's finger foods (the line for the pigs in a blanket can get rather aggressive) and fizzy drinks. I order a Shirley Temple, feeling 'cool' that I'm drinking a drink with a red cherry swirling around the glass. I attempt conversation with a boy who's a couple of years older than me, the son of a family friend. I barely know him beyond small talk, but at 14 years old, I rationalize that we 'shared a moment' earlier in the lobby.

The dining room is one of my cherished spots; I'm one of those people who lives to eat. Saturday night is extra special, and the men at the table talk about ordering the prime rib. I study the menu and decide on the hot pastrami entree.

At 10 PM, we all go to the comedy show in the nightclub. I bask in the fact that I'm staying up late with everyone, and I soak up the Jewish humor the comedian doles out.

———————

We all gather in the lobby, getting ready to leave this place until next winter rolls around again. I wipe my tears away in the car and coax myself not to be too sad on the drive back. When my mother asks if I'm going to miss the people or the place, I say it's both. It's the coming together of the two. Go with the flow are the words written out in my journal. Endings aren't easy, and yet, all good things cease to last.

———————————

Kutshers is now vacant. Most of the resorts in upstate New York have been demolished or transformed, leaving us with spotty remnants of what once was.

Sometimes, I wish to retreat for a few days, and I find myself looking back. I look back to that spot lodged in the Catskill Mountains to a place and time that no longer exists.

5

Body Memories

We drive through the streets of New Paltz, a hippy town that played a prominent role in my freshman year of college. The autumn wind transports me back to Wilklow Orchards.

I would maneuver my way through the orchard as an about-to-be 18-year old, but also as a young girl. I'd grab a pole that was taller than me to reach up into the towering tree, sequestering a Red Delicious or a Macintosh. Before we'd leave the grounds, my parents would buy apple cider doughnuts. Their sugary crystals dissolved on the tip of my tongue.

It's a hazy recollection, but one that leaves me feeling a vague familial longing.

We walk by Fat Bob's. New Paltz is well-known for its eccentric storefronts.

Fat Bobs Pizzeria sold enormous Italian subs—subs with generous layers of Italian meats, topped with provolone cheese and lettuce and tomatoes and black olives and a delicious vinaigrette. My old boyfriend and I couldn't get enough of them. We gobbled them up as if we never ate sandwiches. We'd call for campus delivery and ate on the floor of my dorm room after midnight. Plates and napkins dispersed. Leftovers for the mini fridge.

———————

It's very difficult to remain in that first relationship unscathed. We were young and vulnerable. Love prevailed for three years. Even if it also was my Band-Aid, a way to postpone dealing with my own anxieties.

———————

We walk by the Muddy Cup.

I'd sit with my old boyfriend on a big brown couch at the Muddy Cup, the town's rustic and artsy coffee house; the coffee house where guys would bring their acoustic guitars and where locals smoked cigarettes on the stoop outside. The Muddy Cup kept us snug as we clutched our steaming mugs of coffee and tea. I recall the way in which time stood still for a little. But around 10:30 PM, we had to catch a cab to take us back to where we came from.

———————

The name of the coffee shop is now something else. The name of the pizzeria is now something else, too. But their essences are the same. Funny how people and places tend to do that. Go ahead and change, I say, I still know your core.

———————

The details may surface, but it's not really about them anyway.

———————

We continue our stroll on Main Street.

Main Street once had a jewelry shop that carried precious

stones and crystals; it was where I purchased a green Aventurine candle.

Aventurine benefits all areas of creativity, and imagination, as well as intellect and mental clarity, the label states. It is a gentle stone that gives a sense of calm, balance, and happiness.

Finally, we visit the college. And although I ultimately transferred to another school, it is still surreal to walk through the New Paltz campus and remember the steps I imprinted on that path to that building to that quad back when life was different.

But it's okay that life is different now; it makes sense for it to be.

I think to myself that, again, it's not about a specific recollection or concrete details. This kind of reminiscence conjures up feelings. Feelings in my bones that were previously felt long ago. It's the purity that was upholstered in one moment of time, however fleeting that may have been.

6

The Beginnings

And you, maybe you'll remember me
What I gave is yours to keep
In white houses
—*Vanessa Carlton*

I. My close friend welcomed me into her backyard. Familiar faces said hello; people who I knew from high school but didn't really know. I was identified as "his girlfriend," but what they didn't realize was that he was being distant. However, I beamed at them anyway because the sky was clear and miniature cherries were on my shirt. I really liked cherries. Towels lined the prickly grass. We acquired our first sunburns of the season and chatter filled the thick air. College majors. Summer jobs. Plans for the looming weeks were in the works, and I decided that I would be a part of it. I would belong.

We were no longer together by October, but they still encouraged me to attend the Halloween Party. I somehow managed to talk to people as if my whole world as I knew it wasn't completely shattered. I somehow managed to wear a blonde wig for a photo and watch a weird dance-off in the basement and put cake in my mouth without crying. The crying came in the privacy of my bedroom when I got home. The truth came in Facebook messages when I told people what happened. *Oh, so that's why you seemed off at the Halloween party*, one guy said.

I guess I was transparent after all.

Winter break was spent in that basement. Sometimes, we all talked until four in the morning. Some nights comprised honest conversations about our thoughts and feelings, about where we were at 19 years-old. And some nights comprised conversations about random nothings. We ordered chicken and broccoli dishes from Chinese takeout. We played consecutive games of Uno. Nobody really wanted to say good night, because saying good night meant that we had to go back to our respective houses. We were all searching for companionship, an antidote to loneliness.

II. It was the day after a New Year's Eve bash that set the momentum for the months ahead. Symbolic for the new year. Solace to counter the upcoming days of winter coats and muscles contracting from the cold. I was situated in a new friend group. I'd wear my plaid pajama pants to his house, and we watched lots of movies on weeknights. Weeknights that featured delirium and laughter at one in the morning. I remember thinking that I was fortunate not to have an early wake-up call at an office job in the city.

We had a set routine. For a while, at least. On some nights, Archer would be on the television screen. It wasn't exactly my taste, but I gave it a chance. I gave it all a chance because it's what I needed.

———————

III. Heartbreak was suffocating. I was potentially going to lose a dear friend. I was left hungry for connection, and I just met a group of people. I knew they couldn't save me, but still. They filled the empty spaces with pockets of fuel. With oxygen.

We all gathered at open mic night every week at a small town coffee shop and sang karaoke at the local dive bar. We sang songs from our past. *If I could fall into the sky, do you think time will pass me by? Cause you know, I'd walk a thousand miles, if I can just see you, tonight.*

We binged on episodes of Freaks and Geeks till five am. We had pool parties and played games of pong. (I wasn't very good.) We soared on swings at the elementary school playground under the moonlight. With confided in one another at Point Lookout.

We spent the entire summer together. We helped each other. And I'll never forget that.

I tend to romanticize beginnings. Beginnings are magic. They're comprised of sentimentality and purpose and timing. But some life chapters are supposed to be transient. As days press onward, I notice that those forged connections aren't exactly what I conceived them to be; dynamics change. And that's fine, I suppose.

Those beginnings were still real.

7

The Winter In The West Village

He said he might fall asleep on the train. I said I brought my music. My head rested on his shoulder as the conductor punched two holes in our tickets. We saw black. We were in a tunnel. He said he'd help me with my luggage as we climbed the steps to the outside.

I said the subway is this way. We saw the bustle on 7th Avenue. The shadows on city sidewalks. Feet scurrying. He said the train should be coming. I said the hotel is only a few blocks away from the station. I said I love the charming streets. The village Brownstones. He said to turn this way. We entered the hotel lobby. Art Deco. I gazed out the window on the tenth floor, and I said I'll pretend this is where I live. We said we should take a walk in the neighborhood. I said we should go to Washington Square Park. He said Corner Bistro, famous for their tasty burgers, is nearby.

I said the park is empty at twilight. We were voyeurs as we sat on the fountain steps, and a man blew gigantic bubbles by the arch.

I ogled at the side streets. I said to look at the shops—cheese, records, books, psychics. I said I was overly-stimulated by everything around me. He grinned and said my word choice was interesting.

I said we should turn left, onto a block with an enchanting cathedral. Apparently, it was a synagogue. A man approached us and said a service should be starting soon. He asked if I was Jewish. I said yes, but that I'm not very religious. He asked where we were going. We said we just wanted to eat. He told me to wear a hat. *Girl, it's cold.* I laughed. Loudly. I said okay. We all need armor sometimes.

At 10 PM, I said I was hungry again. He said you're always hungry. In the lobby, we passed women who were sipping on martinis. They were in posh dresses. I chuckled. I said I was the epitome of a slob. Sweatshirt. Pajama pants. Hefty jacket. He said we can go to a hole in the wall pizzeria. One dollar for a slice. I said we shouldn't ask how it's being made. He smirked and said it's better not to ask questions.

We ate our cheese and mushroom slices in the hotel bed and sipped on red wine in plastic cups. I said we can watch Chandler say something hilarious on *Friends*.

———

I said the Saturday rain makes my body feel heavy. Lethargic. We found a French café for brunch. I said I like anything

French. He said the crispy fries dipped in herb aioli mustard will remedy our morning grogginess.

We said we should stay inside because of the weather. At the Met, he said we can check out the modern art exhibit. I asked him for his thoughts. He stood back and studied the surrealism. I said I liked Chagall because it reminded me of a Weepies song. *We float like two lovers in a painting by Chagall.*

We said we were tired. I said we should cut through Central Park on our way back to the subway. The park was quiet, wet, snowy, idyllic, romantic.

He said he wanted to check out The Noodle Shoppe for dinner. The waiter explained the various textures of the noodles. I said I didn't know there were so many. We talked in this old fashioned restaurant with red walls.

Back at the hotel room, we poured wine into our plastic cups, and we wholeheartedly cracked up during *Grease 2*. We said it was so bad, it was good.

————————

In between sips of mimosas and bites of tortilla chips, I said we could relay our personal highlights from the weekend. It was Sunday. I said I wanted to hold onto it all a teensy bit longer.

He said we should come back again as my head rested on his shoulder, and the train moved along the track, back to Long

Island. Further and further away from our wintry weekend in the West Village.

———————

I said this wasn't my first romantic relationship. I said this wasn't my first shot at love. But I also said that this was the first time I glimpsed something real. That after everything I've been through, this was the first glimpse of something that can truly last.

8

Food Is Where The Heart Is

In loving memory of my great-grandmother

Brooklyn, NY

Kibbeh Nabelsieh (Golden Ground Meat-Filled Bulgur Shells) & Zeitoon (Assorted Syrian Olives)

There's a nook on the couch; a nook that everyone desires in the den in the house on East 5th Street with the Spanish-style roof. That block is the heart of the Syrian Jewish Community and five minutes from our apartment building on Ocean Parkway.

We visit, as others often do, my great-grandmother on Saturday afternoons. Planned or impromptu drop-bys. She squeezes us, pinches our skin—her way of saying *I love you*—and immediately offers us food.

Are you hungry?

After the first bite of kibbeh nabelsieh, I sprinkle the meat with lemon juice, savoring the blend of flavors; cumin and paprika and red pepper and kosher salt and a tinge of sour, all embedded within its bulgar wheat shell.

Zeitoon is placed before us as well, oozing with salt and oil and traces of lemon and spice. I like to let its poignant taste linger on my tongue before discarding the pits.

She sits down and asks us what we are up to, sometimes in awe of our age. (After all, she does have several great-grandchildren to keep track of.)

I try to squirm my way into that nook on the couch at some point during our stay. When holidays ensue and all the cousins are here, it quintessentially becomes one cozy nest.

You're so ugly, my great-grandmother says as we say our good-byes. She echoes the same sentiment to my brother, too, and we can't help but giggle because if you know her, you know what she really means. That we are nothing short of *gorgeous*.

Djaj Mishwi (Roast Chicken And Potatoes)

Every year, Passover seders are conducted in the dining room, which can seat approximately 30 dinner guests. White curtains majestically drape over the cushioned benches in the back; a portrait of my great-grandmother's father-in-law hangs on the mahogany wood paneling. He was a highly-respected man in the community; he was a cantor in the synagogue and wrote celebratory religious songs.

In between reading each passage, spirited banter fills the room; a testament to the company we keep.

My great-grandmother is deeply rooted in tradition, in Sephardic customs, and she ensures that the holiday rituals are followed. I glance over at her from time to time, noting her composed elegance, her delicate stoicism.

Once the haroset (Syrian-style haroset is comprised of dates instead of apples and is spread over matzah) is placed on the table, we know we are a step closer to the 'festive meal.'

Djaj mishwi is a featured entree and Poopa Dweck, author of Aromas of Aleppo, The Legendary Cuisine of Syrian Jews, writes: "The potatoes in this dish are fried before they are added to the chicken. After absorbing the pan drippings, they become absolutely addictive. When the chicken is done roasting, one tradition is to cut it into eighths and serve it layered among the potatoes."

And today, two days after her memorial service and a month after she passed, I become acutely aware that I may never be in that Brooklyn home again. But you know, it's not really about the house.

It's really about Grandma. And it's not the same without her there.

Deal, New Jersey

Spanekh b'Jibn (Spinach-Cheese Frittata) & Sambousak (Buttery Cheese-Filled Sesame Pastries):

I smell the Atlantic Ocean as we drive up to the entrance of the condominium and unload our bags. My great-grandmother waits for us downstairs in the lavish lobby where the sun emits a golden glow across the white marble floor. When we go upstairs to her apartment on the second floor, our feet walk across a smooth, floral-patterned carpet.

We *ooh* and *ahh* over the exquisite lunch she prepares for us at the small kitchen table, and we catch up on our lives, on family and community and condominium updates, near the window that overlooks a quiet street near the water and a quaint church on the corner.

Spanekh b'jibn—a lightly browned quiche without the pie crust—melts in my mouth with its melted muenster cheese intertwined with spinach and chopped onion and egg. Sambousak—buttery sesame pastries filled with melted Muenster cheese—is another Syrian delight that's typically served during a midday meal or snack.

After we finish whatever's left on our plates, we make our way to the guest room. Out comes the sunscreen, the bathing suits, the noodles.

I'll meet you downstairs and sit at the pool, she tells us. *Let me get ready.*

My great-grandmother is a social butterfly, admired in the community, adored and beloved by friends.

Laham b'ajeen (Miniature Tamarind Minced Meat Pies) & Rice with Keftes (Tamarind-Stewed Meatballs) & Yebra (Stuffed Grape Leaves with Apricots and Prunes):

I persistently comb through the knots in my hair after I shower and wash off the chlorine from my body. I stare at my reflection in the mirror, tan lines and a little burnt, refreshed from an afternoon of swimming and traipsing around the beach, the fiery sand burning my toes.

I can already smell the Friday night meal that's to come; my great-uncle and cousin arrive for Shabbat Dinner, too, and we sit in the living room as we wait.

Some kibbeh is ready to hold you over, my mom tells me.

My great-grandmother stands with us for the blessings; we tear off bits of challah bread and pass them down so everyone gets a piece. And then, we eat.

Grandma, are you going to sit down? my mom asks.

And she will. But for now, she still retreats to and from the kitchen, checking on the meat, on the assorted courses.

Laham b'ajeen—mini Syrian meat pies with a strong, tangy flavor, cooked with lemons, tamarind concentrate, ground allspice, kosher salt, and tomato paste—were served before the meal but are still part of the dinner spread, along with djaj mishwi, her famous white rice and keftes (a delectable tomato and tamarind meatball sauce), yebra, grape leaves stuffed with ground meat and rice, and a salad with crisp lettuce, ripe tomatoes, and a light vinaigrette.

"Yebra is the distinctively Aleppian version of the popular Mediterranean stuffed grape leaves," Dweck writes. "Instead of using the lemon and garlic that accents the common Mediterranean version, Aleppian Jews flavor yebra with dried apricots and tamarind concentrate. The Aleppian Jews' penchant for tangy and fruity dishes betrays the Persian influence on their cuisine. Unlike lemon-garlic stuffed grape leaves, which are almost always cooked on the stove top and are often served cold, yebra is served hot and may be cooked slowly in the oven to allow the apricots to melt and the ou (tamarind concentrate) to absorb into the hashu (the meat and rice filling)."

Baklawa (Pistachio Filla Wedges in Rose Water Syrup):

After dinner, we lounge in the living room; a room where sophistication is juxtaposed with comfort; a room with serene, salmon-colored walls. A small statue of Buddha is on the black coffee table—my great-grandfather traveled to China on business. My great-grandmother tells us stories about their life together, about her past. She's seen a lot, endured a lot, survived a lot. Her voice could be likened to a lullaby, melodic and intimate.

With a lengthy scrabble game ahead of us and a Mets baseball game muted on television, she serves dessert, even though our stomachs are still quite full.

Eat, she insists.

I nibble on (parve) cake, fruit, and baklawa, a pistachio, syrup-filled pastry, that's cut into little diamond shapes. The delicate filla is quick to crumble; this isn't the neatest dessert to eat, but sometimes, the messier, the better.

I peer at my grandmother, renowned for her sweet tooth, as she compiles her own small plate of treats, patiently awaiting her turn in our scrabble game. She's in it for the long haul.

Jibneh Shelal (Twisted White String Cheese with Nigella Seeds) & Ka'ak (Savory Anise-Seed Rings):

When the guest room is occupied, I sleep in my great-grand-mother's bed, though she turns in before me. The master bedroom captures her essence—graceful, polished, tranquil.

She drifts off to sleep with the television on low volume. I lie in bed listening to the hushed tones of news anchors, of *The Cosby Show;* sometimes, she wakes up and changes the channel.

When the sunlight pierces through the window, I know her side of the bed will be empty. It's still early, but she's up to start breakfast, to drink her coffee in solitude.

I make my way to the kitchen after everyone else; my cousin is already downstairs by the pool, perhaps indulging in an early swim, perhaps delving into one of her books.

And though I typically don't have a hearty appetite for breakfast, it's hard to resist smoked salmon (lox), jibneh shelal, twisted white string cheese with black nigella seeds, also known as "black cumin," and ka'ak, seeded-crackers that can be dipped in coffee.

"Ka'ak has the texture and crunch of a breadstick, but it is ring-shaped with a crimped edge," Dweck notes. "A staple of the Aleppian pantry, ka'ak is usually offered to guests when Aleppian Jews serve coffee or tea."

How did you sleep? my grandmother asks as I pick apart string after string of Syrian cheese.

I tell her I slept well, and before we know it, she's discussing what she'll put out for lunch.

You really don't need to worry about lunch, my mom chimes in. *Maybe we can go to the coffee shop today?*

Okay, she replies. You can see she's itching to say more, though, and then out it adamantly comes: *I'll give you spanekh to take home.*

When the visits to Deal stopped, I felt it. I felt a little bit of a hole. Or maybe it was just a little bit of innocence being chipped away, which definitely tends to happen as we get older.

Though my great-grandmother is no longer here, she's with me in every bite of Syrian food. She's with me in every thought of Brooklyn and Deal. She's with me in every bit of truth that she will be missed.

9

Back In Brooklyn

A light wind blew through the Brooklyn air that September afternoon. The September afternoon where autumn's fickleness made its presence known. We were in the midst of seasonal transition when I saw my old apartment building in my old neighborhood. The sun's intensity bore down on my bare shoulders.

The building's awning shed its green for a cranberry red, and the furniture in the lobby was arranged differently. Still, my dad and I decided to explore the familiar; to visit our old apartment on the first floor.

Our apartment was unique in that it featured an outdoor patio, which gave me and my younger brother ample opportunities for recreation; we played basketball with our (fisher price) hoop, dashed through sprinklers in the August heat, and hit whiffle balls against the brick wall. We ran around our turf, making noise, while notably angering the elderly woman who lived alone in the apartment above. Her gaze met ours, and her eyes conveyed disappointment. My mother told her that we were just kids. We just wanted to play.

I could recall being a young girl in our apartment, and how I would dart across the outstretched hallway, the hallway with a black and white floor pattern, that led to my parents' bedroom. Sometimes the running was part of an improvised game, our own built-in personal track, but sometimes it was instigated from a bad dream. I'd wake up from a nightmare in the middle of the night, and I'd speed down the hall to seek relief in my mother's embrace.

And then there was my bedroom; a shared space with my brother. It's where I listened to music (NSYNC), wrote in my diary, played with Barbie dolls, hung my Spice Girls posters, and huddled under the covers on nights when fear got the best of me.

My room had a carpet that was blue. An ocean blue that instilled a sense of liveliness and calm.

———————

We buzzed ourselves in, wondering if the family now living in our old apartment would understand that we were just two people looking to see what's no longer ours. A kind-hearted man let us upstairs and greeted us at the door mat. He was sweating. He explained that he's newly retired and therefore has the opportunity to go jogging. Good for him, I thought. A path, utilized by joggers and bikers, is across the street from the building. I attempted to learn how to ride a bike on that path, but I was too scared of falling. I taught myself on our patio, on my own terms.

As we walked into the apartment, the man wiped the sweat from his brow and invited us to sit down at the dining room table. We thanked him, profusely, but relayed that we only desired to stop in.

The black and white floor pattern along the hallway was gone and the patio was bare.

Yet, the layout was still recognizable and memories inevitably surfaced. That wall behind the table, adjacent to the kitchen, is where all of our elementary school artwork was displayed. Here's the living room where I used to sing into a plastic microphone and dance to that Paul McCartney song: *There never could be a better moment, than this one, this one.*

The kind-hearted man gave us a tour of the apartment in its entirety; he genuinely wanted to do so, but he also gathered that it meant something.

And then we approached my old bedroom.

I saw a carpet that was blue.

It was the color of the ocean.

And I smiled.

Because some things never change. Because I was back inside my childhood home. Back to where it all began. Back to where pieces of me are found. Pieces that would then scatter, finding a home in places and people; in phases of life.

About the Author

Lauren Suval is a writer based in Long Island, NY. After studying print journalism and psychology at Hofstra University, she freelanced for Psych Central, writing editorial-based articles for their World of Psychology Blog. In recent years, she began experimenting with short fictional and nonfictional narratives as well, and her pieces have been featured on *Thought Catalog, Medium, Catapult Community,* and other online publications. Her e-book, "Coping With Life's Clutter," was self-published on Amazon in the fall of 2014.

"The Art Of Nostalgia," her latest work, is a collection of nine personal essays, and it's a collection that's very close to her heart. After all, those who know Lauren, generally know that 'nostalgia' may as well be her middle name.

About the Author

www.ingramcontent.com/pod-product-compliance
Lightning Source LLC
Chambersburg PA
CBHW021146020426
42331CB00005B/927